A high-performance team is like a well-oiled machine.

Each team member has a specific role.

Each possesses complementary talents and skills.

Every person understands, aligns with

and is committed to a common purpose.

Individually, and as a group, members consistently show

high levels of collaboration, innovation and trust.

Together they produce superior results.

The Manager's
High-Performance
Handbook

Printed in the United States of America.

13-digit ISBN: 978-1-885228-14-7

Credits

Copy Editor	Kathleen Green, Positively Proofed, Plano, TX info@PositivelyProofed.com
Design, art direction & production	Melissa Cabana, Back Porch Creative, Plano, TX info@BackPorchCreative.com
Interior graphics	Tim Cocklin, Worlds of Wonder Studios, Garland, TX Tim@WorldsofWonderStudios.com
Cover graphic	© iStockPhoto.com

Introduction

It's Friday afternoon. Your boss calls you into her office to discuss the team's performance, and she looks serious.

She tells you, "Right now our actions aren't producing the results that are needed. Now, more than ever, we need to be achieving our targets. We have this quarter to improve our outcomes before leadership starts looking at our department and making some tough decisions."

After a pause, she adds, "We have to find a way to improve our results, especially with your team. Over the weekend, let's think about what we can do to drive performance, fix any shortcomings and quickly get that impact."

You know that your boss values you and the work you do. You know you have a talented team, but performance can improve. Each member must produce results and be engaged.

You need breakthrough results instead of more breakdowns. And, based on your boss's remarks, you need to drive that higher performance quickly.

When you lead team members with high potential and they don't perform, it can be frustrating. In many ways, it's like owning a high-performance race car that only operates in low gear. The car has the capability to win, but the pit crew can't make it work properly and get it back in the race.

As a leader, your job is to inspire your own crew to focus on performance, make improvements, negotiate roadblocks and drive results where possible. You need to diagnose any possible issues with operations, strategy or your environment that could cause problems.

Imagine the opportunities that would result if your team members systematically and consistently performed at their highest level every day.

Whether you lead two people or 200, this book is designed to help you improve performance and obtain winning outcomes. You'll see approaches to accelerate your success and warning indicators to help you avoid problems. Specifically, you'll find practical tips to help you and your team:

1. Attract, qualify and select motivated people with the right talents.

2. Understand, align and commit to a common purpose.

3. Build high levels of collaboration, innovation and trust.

4. Focus on and produce superior results.

The solutions provided in this book are based on 25 years of helping high-performing leaders achieve results in a variety of roles and organizations. Also, ideas come from survey results of more than 800 professionals who shared their experiences and best practices on achieving high performance.

In every chapter, you'll be able to test your leadership strategy and identify specific tune-up areas to focus your efforts. In addition, you'll be able to create a personal high-performance action plan to help you maintain performance and drive winning results.

Are you ready to improve your leadership and your team's performance?

If so, buckle up.

Start your engines.

And get ready to fast-track your journey to high performance and winning results.

Contents

*Desire is the key to motivation, but it's
determination and commitment to an
unrelenting pursuit of your goal –
a commitment to excellence – that will
enable you to attain the success you seek.*

– **Mario Andretti**,
Formula One legend and author of
*Race to Win: How to Become a
Complete Champion Driver*

Locate High Performers

High performers share similar attitudes and behaviors. They are motivated, dedicated self-starters who adapt, no matter the circumstances. Their energy is contagious and engaging. Adding the right people to your team makes all the difference. However, you first must find them, qualify them and choose them.

Find Performers

When you are seeking high performers for your team, look at two groups:

1. Team members now in the group who need to be developed.

2. Candidates outside your team whom you need to invite to join.

Performers On Your Current Team

Currently, you may have people on your team who could perform at a higher level. Look around. Often these talented people serve as informal leaders. They are mentoring others and producing extraordinary results.

There are great reasons to look to your existing employees.

First, their learning curves concerning the organization, your processes and their new roles are much shorter than someone joining from the outside.

Second, you don't need to teach them about the team or your organizational culture or structure, because they belong. They already know the procedures and can access information quickly.

Third, promoting internally encourages loyalty and demonstrates that hard work is recognized and rewarded. You show you develop and grow your current talent first.

Finally, there may be qualified people working on a different team or even in a different location. Often, you can tap them for help without additional cost. Borrowing or leveraging underutilized performers reflects innovation and resourcefulness, plus it prevents having to ask leadership for additional resources.

Applicants Outside Your Team

If internal candidates aren't available and the job has approved funding, consider all your options to acquire people outside your organization. Typically managers wait for future employees to apply for a posted job. Some applicants are recruited to gain industry knowledge and expertise.

However, you may want to broaden your search efforts. Ask your team members about people they know. Your best want to work with the best. Qualified candidates are frequently suggested by high performers.

Also, you may work with candidates who already understand your culture and the work your team does. A great intern or a temporary worker can be a good addition. If there isn't an agreement preventing it, business partners (*e.g.* vendors, clients or contractors) offer a pool of qualified candidates.

There may be available people who have experience with your organization. For instance, tap into your "alums." People who left your group may be ready to return. Alums bring a new appreciation for the work as well as new skills to contribute.

In addition, consider those with gaps in their employment history. People returning to work after a break may have desirable qualities, including talent *and* a dedication to work. Oftentimes, candidates who experienced a layoff are committed to performing well in their next job.

Absence from employment doesn't always signal a problem. A leave due to a military obligation or deployment signals a person willing to go the extra mile. And don't reject those who took time to raise children or care for a sick family member. Devoting time to family displays loyalty, caring and selflessness.

Qualify the Right People

To qualify high-performing candidates, your interviews will serve two purposes. First, you are checking abilities and for a fit with your organization and team. Second, you are determining the candidate's history and desire or bias for achieving performance.

The first purpose of an interview is to determine if applicants have the basic "abilities" required for the role and team.

Candidates must possess the skills, talent, education, experience and basic relationship talents needed.

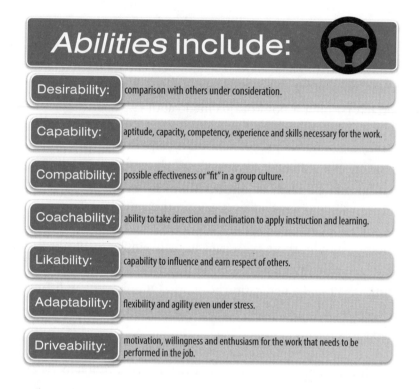

Abilities include:

Desirability: comparison with others under consideration.

Capability: aptitude, capacity, competency, experience and skills necessary for the work.

Compatibility: possible effectiveness or "fit" in a group culture.

Coachability: ability to take direction and inclination to apply instruction and learning.

Likability: capability to influence and earn respect of others.

Adaptability: flexibility and agility even under stress.

Driveability: motivation, willingness and enthusiasm for the work that needs to be performed in the job.

Qualify on Performance and Possibility to Perform

The second purpose of an interview is often overlooked. As a leader, you want to determine whether an applicant has a record of performance or could perform if given the opportunity. Technical skills, education, similar work experience and appearance are important. When hiring or promoting performers, employers look for people who:

■ Possess a positive attitude and get along well with others.

■ Are self-starters.

■ Know how to solve problems.

■ Show a proven ability to communicate.

Interview Questions to Hire Performers

Answers to these open-ended questions will help you determine which candidates possess the history, beliefs and desire for achieving high performance.

1. Describe a time you worked under pressure. How did you handle the stress?

2. Tell me about a time you failed, and it wasn't your fault.

3. How do you handle a co-worker who will not do his or her fair share of the work?

4. Give me an example of a process, project or idea you presented that was implemented.

5. Describe a time you had to complete a difficult project but were not provided the resources you wanted or needed to complete it. What was the outcome?

Pay special attention to what is said and how it is said during interviews. A candidate's body language, especially a change when responding to different questions, can indicate uneasiness and/or that you need to ask more questions for clarification or understanding.

Choose and Promote the Right Talent

When given a choice, choose candidates who actively grew their expertise and enhanced their knowledge throughout their careers. This dedication to growth is a greater predictor of high performers than references and longevity in a position.

Surprisingly, references ranked last in hiring decisions among those surveyed! Likewise, the length of time spent in a position doesn't always predict future performance. Some survey responders even suggested longevity in a role might reflect a lack of initiative.

Choose People With Positive Attitudes

Performers possess a positive attitude and get along well with others. Attitude is one key to performance. You can teach and help develop skills, but you can't "teach" positive attitude. Spend your efforts developing people who:

- Pitch in when their peers get stuck or need help.

- Are willing and able to explain processes to others.

- Show courtesy to vendors and outside providers.

- Respond to a customer's complaint with respect.

- Find the positive even when faced with challenges.

Armed with a positive attitude, self-starters are a joy to work with and upgrade their teams and employers.

Qualify Candidates With Current Performers' Help

Your hiring decisions impact your team. Your current performers know what it takes to do the job and how someone new could enhance the team's efforts. Enlist the input of those performers to help you select the right members for the team. Consider asking them to:

- Help you identify the type of skills or talents the team is missing.

- Provide you with questions that relate to actual job requirements.

- Participate in interviews.

- Hold separate team interviews with candidates.

- Give you feedback on what they observed during the interviews.

Choose Self-Starters

Self-starters determine what is important, ask the necessary questions and quickly get into action. They are flexible, take calculated risks and make good decisions. Identify self-starters on your team to hire, develop and promote.

Avoid Stallers Who Delay Work

When choosing team members, watch out for "stallers" who postpone decisions, delay work and fail to solve problems. Stallers wait for direction, for permission and for someone else to do the task or thinking for them. Avoid those who say:

"It isn't my job."

"No one told me to do it."

"I didn't know it was important."

"I wondered about that, but I didn't know if I should act."

Stallers are close-minded. They refuse new ideas, don't work well in a team and confuse issues. They complicate your leadership, results and life.

Self-starters	Stallers will:
Quickly get into action.	Passively wait for instructions.
Determine the importance of tasks.	Have difficulty prioritizing.
Ask questions to clarify.	Remain silent to avoid looking stupid or to decrease workload.
Be flexible, agile and adapt well.	Be rigid and resist change.
Take calculated risks.	Possess a low risk tolerance.
Be results-oriented.	Exhibit a strong desire for status quo.
Seek and take responsibility.	Avoid responsibility.
Make the best decisions in the moment.	Postpone decisions until made by another or forced to choose.
Solve problems when encountered.	Ignore issues and problems and only follow defined procedures.

If you have stallers draining your team's performance, decide how to invest your energy in them. In some cases, you may determine the stallers no longer need to work with your team or for your organization.

Choose Problem Solvers

When given a choice, pick proactive problem *solvers* not problem *creators*. Problem solvers know how to ask for help and seek clarification when appropriate.

When adding people to your team, identify those who:

- Focus their attention on actual problems instead of being distracted by drama.
- Strive to understand the situation or another's point of view.
- Look for a resolution without blaming others for the problems.
- Create solutions instead of depending on others to think for them.
- Accept responsibility for solving issues and resolving mistakes whether they made them or not.
- Stay cool, calm and in control despite a difficult situation or person.

Avoid Complainers and Energy Drainers

High-performing teams make it a practice to avoid constant complainers or energy drainers. Complainers are poor communicators, selfish and blame others for their problems. In interviews, these negative people tend to criticize past employers, leaders and peers.

When asked about personal weaknesses or negative outcomes, they don't take responsibility. They divide teams and pit people against each other. No matter their expertise or education, do not invite these energy drainers or their problems to your team.

Choose Proven Communicators

To accelerate your existing team's performance, consider communications training. Fast-track your efforts by seeking and promoting people who already possess a proven ability to communicate. Even the most highly educated people can fail to get a message across or relate to other team members.

Half of survey respondents said communication is the skill people need to learn or develop for the most significant change in high performance.

Choose communicators who write well, speak well and relate well to others. A good communicator:

- Smiles and makes eye contact.

- Has a firm handshake and is polite.

- Develops presentation skills.

- Works on clarity of speech.

- Uses proper grammar, spelling and language.

- Responds in a timely manner to emails and calls.

- Allows others to speak and share thoughts.

- Stays relevant and shares relevant information.

- Asks questions, listens and obtains feedback.

To accelerate your existing team's performance, consider communications training. Fast-track your efforts by seeking and promoting people who already possess a proven ability to communicate. Even the most highly educated people can fail to get a message across or relate to other team members.

■ ■ ■ ■ ■

High-Performance Dashboard:
Locate High Performers

The secret to winning results is to find, qualify and choose performers. Seek and identify people who have complementary talents and skills combined with a drive to produce results.

 Gauge how well you are locating high performers by answering below on a scale of 1-5 (5 being highest).

When seeking high performers, I

_____ Consider people inside and outside my existing team.

_____ Determine candidates' *abilities,* including Desirability, Capability, Compatibility, Coachability, Likability, Agility and Driveability.

_____ Ask open-ended questions to determine candidates' history, beliefs and desires for achieving high performance.

_____ Involve my current performers to help me add the right people with the right talent to our team.

_____ Choose people with positive attitudes who are self-starters, problem solvers and have a proven ability to communicate.

Total "Locate High Performers" Score (Insert this score on your High-Performance Dashboard on page 57.)

Your High-Performance Action Plan

To improve my performance score, I need to:

_____

_____

_____

_____

It's a never-ending battle of
making your cars better and
also trying to be better yourself.

– **Dale Earnhardt**,
"The Intimidator,"
award-winning race-car driver,
owner and NASCAR Hall of Famer

Align With a Common Purpose & Operating Practices

High-performing teams understand and commit to a common purpose and operating practices. In doing so, they create a supportive environment where each member is valued, trusted and encouraged. Together they are more likely to reach greater outcomes than what is possible on their own.

Performance improves because members recognize how their work and results impact the overall organization. They understand the reasons they are working together. And team members know how they fit and are able to contribute.

Mission Statements
Many organizations have statements to describe their strategic mission and direction to marketplace. For instance:

Mayo Clinic: To inspire hope and contribute to health and well-being by providing the best care to every patient through integrated clinical practice, education and research.

Southwest Airlines: Dedication to the highest quality of customer service with a sense of warmth, friendliness, individual pride, and company spirit.

San Diego Zoo Global: Committed to saving species worldwide by uniting our expertise in animal care and conservation science with our dedication to inspiring passion for nature.

Girl Scouts: Builds girls of courage, confidence, and character, who make the world a better place.

Meaningful, organization-wide statements are not specific enough to define a team's objectives and daily tasks. Smart leaders recognize that it is important to develop teams as operational groups guided by purpose statements, which describe why they exist and specifically what they do.

Understand Your Team's Common Purpose

Whether your team drafts its own statement or a purpose has been provided for your group, it should define the "who," "what" and "why" of the work to be accomplished. A good purpose statement is usually 25 words or less and helps people know the reasons the team exists.

High-performing teams have purpose statements, such as:

- We provide quality, caring and professional health services that our physicians, our patients and our patients' families can trust.

- We provide best-in-class project management. Our people, tools and processes deliver quality, on-schedule services with strong margins.

- The training and development we provide enables our colleagues to obtain a competitive advantage over any global-services provider.

There are no standard or "one size fits all" purpose statements. Instead, each is meaningful to the team performing the work. Once you have a successful purpose statement, it is apparent. Everyone considers the words and shows acceptance. Usually, people nod and make comments like: "Yes. That's what we do." "We nailed it." Or "That sums it up. I wouldn't change a thing."

Developing a clear understanding of the team's purpose is essential. However, high-performing teams also need operating practices, which define the way team members think, act and believe when working with each other.

Lead With Operating Practices

Operating practices are the principles, behaviors and values that the team uses to function on a daily basis. They clearly define how team members behave when relating to or engaging with one another.

As a leader, sit down with your group to determine what you want and don't want as a team. Remember, your people are more likely to support what they help create, so involve all team members. Examples of behavior that team members *don't* want may be easiest to determine first.

On our team, we do not tolerate:

- Gossip, lying or dishonesty.
- Shifting blame or finger pointing.
- Rudeness or disrespectful behavior.
- Unnecessary excuses or ignoring problems.
- Unethical activities.
- Inflexible attitudes.
- Withholding information or insight from others.
- Selfishness or lack of concern for others.

Here are samples of practices valued by high-performing team members.

In our team, we:

- Respect the knowledge and contributions of others.
- Are willing to grow and to adapt.
- Commit to every team member's success.
- Help other teams and departments.
- Have a "can do" problem-solving attitude.
- Take responsibility.
- Trust each other.
- Celebrate each other's victories.
- Take great care of our internal and external clients/customers.
- Pitch in and go beyond expectations.
- Encourage open communication and collaboration.
- Allow for mistakes and manage emotions.

When your team determines the practices they want, you'll hear statements like: "Hey, we already do this." Or "Where do I sign up? I'm in." Or "These are no-brainers. Of course we want to work that way."

You may want to revisit the strategies in Chapter 1 to ensure you are locating candidates who support your team's common purpose and operating practices.

Drive Common Purpose and Operating Practices

As a leader, you can continue to drive commitment to the team's purpose and operating practices in several ways:

- Show the purpose and operating practices to candidates and ask for their promise to uphold the team's values before they join.

- Post a document or a sign reflecting the team's purpose and practices.

- During team meetings, examine how proposed solutions, actions or projects reflect the team's purpose and operating practices.

- Ask for examples of when the purpose or practices are demonstrated.

- Hold members accountable in their performance reviews or coaching sessions for actions according to the team's purpose or practices.

- Recognize and reward people whose actions reflect the team's purpose.

- On a regular basis, review the practices with the group to determine if they are still relevant or if any should be added or revised.

Team Members Drive Their Own Behavior

Dramatic improvement in team performance happens when managers and members focus on their operating practices. Clear team practices make your job as a leader easier because your people can monitor themselves. Instead of managing basic rules of respect and policing professionalism, your daily focus can shift to leading others in achieving goals, concentrating on objectives and producing high-performance results.

Interestingly, if your team's purpose and practices are publicized, people may choose not to belong. Low performers may decide not to join a team with high standards they can't uphold. They may choose to leave a team voluntarily instead of conforming or reforming their behavior. Their self-selection is good news for you as a leader and prevents you from wasting valuable time and effort.

■   ■   ■   ■   ■

High-Performance Dashboard:
Common Purpose & Operating Practices

The secret to winning results is to have everyone on your team understand, align with and commit to a common purpose and operating practices.

 Gauge how well you drive your team's purpose and practices by answering below on a scale of 1-5 (5 being highest).

To help others understand our team's common purpose and operating practices, I

_____ Review our common purpose with new members and gain their commitment to uphold our operating practices before joining our team.

_____ Hold people accountable for their actions according to our team's common purpose and operating practices.

_____ Consider our purpose and operating practices in discussions and during meetings, especially before making decisions involving our team.

_____ Recognize and reward members whose actions reflect our purpose and practices.

_____ Make sure my words, decisions and actions reflect our team's purpose and practices.

Total "Common Purpose & Operating Practices" Score (Insert this score on your High-Performance Dashboard on page 57.)

Your High-Performance Action Plan

To improve my performance score, I need to:

_____

_____

_____

_____

If you don't have enough faith
in your crew, car and your ability
you shouldn't be out here.

– Shirley Muldowney,
first woman of drag racing

Drive Team Collaboration & Innovation

Within seconds, a pit crew can change tires, refuel a gas tank, make minor adjustments to a car and have a driver ready to re-enter the track. Like the crew, high-performing teams work together like a well-oiled machine. Individually and as a group, performers show strong collaboration and innovation.

Teams won't trust each other or work successfully together if they are unclear about the direction, strategy or people's roles. Your people must be clear about where their organization is headed and what is expected from them by upper management. As the leader, the most effective ways to get people and teams to work successfully toward a common goal or direction are to:

■ Provide clear directions and hold people accountable.

■ Communicate strategy from leadership.

- Develop a high level of trust.

- Understand everyone's role.

Clarify Direction

Most people need clear directions and accountability before they can work effectively together. When direction is vague, people are left to create their own interpretations and determine priorities. Therefore, the leader and organization's expectations aren't met. In addition, people are frustrated and everyone wastes time and energy.

Occasionally, you'll find people comfortable working with ambiguity. However, more than 75 percent of our survey respondents said they want clear directions and accountability.

As a leader, the most effective ways to provide clear directions and hold others accountable are to:

- Set clear expectations of tasks to be performed and desired outcomes.

- Evaluate your people's performance based on expectations.

- Measure results and know when results are not occurring.

- Create a process to help people diagnose and correct when issues occur or things aren't working to plan.

- Provide regular and candid feedback.

- Acknowledge and give people credit for their contribution.

- Regularly review outcomes to ensure members are producing what is required and what they promised.

- Monitor to ensure team members are not overburdened and taking on more than they committed to do.

Communicate Strategy From Leadership

Organizational objectives and periodic communication from upper management are not enough to drive high performance. As a leader, make sure to communicate your organization's strategy and share how your team's efforts fit into the bigger goals. When people understand the reasons they perform work, their results improve and your team is more dedicated to the strategy. Also, team members are more likely to interact with other groups in a meaningful way and make decisions to accomplish objectives logically.

Develop a High Level of Trust

Driving performance requires more than communicating strategy and providing clear directions. Trust accelerates performance and makes your life as a leader easier. Great leaders surround themselves with people they trust on several levels.

How trustworthy are the people around you? Can you:

Trust their capabilities? High performers know the need for possessing competitive skills and expertise. When needed, they seek personal development, including self-study, as well as coaching or training to learn new skills and to keep them current. They know whom they can trust to gain reliable insight.

Trust their decisions? High performers know the importance of dependability and having others rely on their judgment. They pay special attention to accurate information, provide valid data, and can access reliable contacts.

Trust their integrity? High performers know the value of honesty. They don't cheat – even if no one would know – or lie – even when news isn't pleasant.

Trust them to maintain confidences and sensitive information? High performers know that releasing trade secrets, client data or sensitive personnel issues hurts organizations.

Drive a Higher Level of Trust

Here are ideas to accelerate a higher level of trust in your team:

- Recognize those who stay current in their expertise.

- Support team members who wish to seek additional training to increase knowledge or improve a skill.

- Introduce them to your trusted advisors.

- Encourage them to seek their teammates' opinions and insight.

- Identify who is trusted and relied upon by his or her peers.

- Have members shadow or train others in their function and roles.

- Partner members on projects to acquaint them with each other's talents, skills and reliability.

High performers also value trustworthiness in their peers. Trust is enhanced by defining and appreciating each member's role.

Understand Roles

Teams are less likely to idle and delay action if they have knowledge of what everyone on the team does and how each role serves to drive results. Visibility of roles helps clear up assumptions and prevent confusion.

Race to Performance with RACI

High-performing teams use a responsibility matrix or "RACI" chart when there are a number of people involved in the completion of a task or in the making of a decision. A RACI chart defines who is **R**esponsible, **A**ccountable, **C**onsulted and **I**nformed. Like a dashboard, a RACI chart clarifies expectations, participation and roles required. Basically, RACI shows who does what, with whom and when.

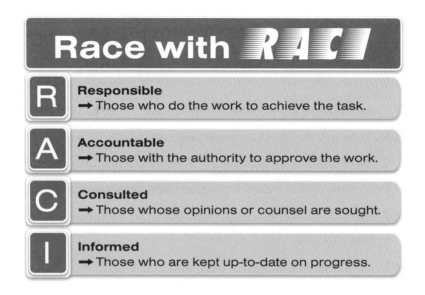

Race with **RACI**

R
Responsible
→ Those who do the work to achieve the task.

A
Accountable
→ Those with the authority to approve the work.

C
Consulted
→ Those whose opinions or counsel are sought.

I
Informed
→ Those who are kept up-to-date on progress.

Inspire High Levels of Collaboration

Team members who know and trust each other's capabilities, decisions and integrity multiply their influence and outcomes. Collaboration is one of the keys to effectively use your organizational knowledge.

Many teams work independently or in "silos." In silos, members of the same organization don't pool knowledge, effectively use resources or even communicate well. When challenges and best practices aren't shared among different groups, it causes confusion, wasted time and duplication of effort.

Instead, direct your team members to reach out to their peers in other groups for insight into processes, to understand issues or to gain additional resources.

Drive Collaboration

High performers are always reaching out to others for help and to help. Give people the chance to provide input, grow, think creatively and stretch beyond their daily duties. Encourage your members to reach out when they want to:

- Seek knowledge when they are inexperienced in a particular area.

- Generate ideas to form a more complete solution.

- Gain direction at the onset or opinions on how to proceed.

- Include stakeholders or others affected by the decisions or results.

- Fine-tune, identify gaps or explore other options.

- Avoid unintended consequences and make adjustments before a negative result occurs.

- Engage others, foster teamwork and enlist support.

- Gain agreement, seek cooperation and build alliances.

- Ask for help before the situation becomes overwhelming.

Remember, the power of collaboration and openly seeking feedback must be demonstrated by the leader. Let team members see you assist your peers and ask for help. Show how you involve others in your decision making.

Create a Safe Approach to Ask for Help

There is a risk to reaching out, especially when you don't know the answer. Your people may have a legitimate fear that others will judge them or they'll receive bad advice. Make collaboration safer by encouraging your people to:

- Pick advisors who have their best interests at heart.

- Find "safe" people to answer questions without judgment.
- Seek knowledge and honest feedback from high performers or subject-matter experts.

Encourage Innovation

You and your team need agility to take advantage of opportunities and to react to setbacks. Your members may have a solution but not the confidence to act. Ask them for suggestions and creative help. Even if you don't think you need or will use the input, asking it is worth the effort. Responses you receive may result in insightful ideas; plus, members feel more empowered and included.

Often, people innovate when you give them time and an issue to solve. Make it a practice to have your team analyze what works and what could be improved on a project or a process. Once your team knows innovating is part of their work responsibility, they start proposing solutions to the problems they spot.

Perform a Team Diagnostic

Ask your team to do a "diagnostic" on their team. Have members examine the team's current effectiveness. Ask them to diagnose what areas of innovation are needed to upgrade the team's performance. Below is a sample format.

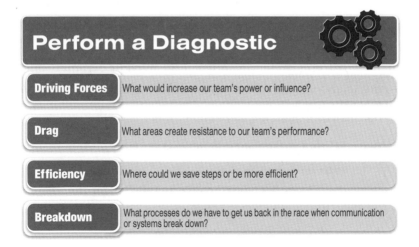

Perform a Diagnostic

Driving Forces	What would increase our team's power or influence?
Drag	What areas create resistance to our team's performance?
Efficiency	Where could we save steps or be more efficient?
Breakdown	What processes do we have to get us back in the race when communication or systems break down?

The results of an analysis can reveal precise areas where changes, upgrades and solutions are needed. Be prepared for high-speed, innovative suggestions.

Boost Innovation

Look for people who spark ideas, collaborate and make your life as a leader easier. The ways to boost innovation include asking team members to:

- Lead a project.

- Present a key part of a presentation.

- Shadow another leader.

- Be a shift or team leader.

- Give their ideas or thoughts on an issue.

- Attend a meeting *for* you. Attend meetings *with* you.

High Performers are Innovators

Your high performers have the ability to innovate and generate creative solutions if they know what areas need upgrading or repair. When you expose them to issues and challenges, you encourage a higher level of thinking, problem solving and innovating.

Consider bringing team members to meetings with your boss or peers, especially those that involve strategic decisions. Attending gives them an up-front perspective of your job and a bigger picture of what is expected from the team by your organization. Your people also gain insight regarding the expectations placed on you and other leaders.

Keep Your High Performers Engaged

High performers have a proven track record to deliver results on a consistent basis. They are your "go to" people to get the job done quickly, effectively and with little supervision.

Often, performers prove themselves, obtain outstanding results and aren't rewarded for it. People with talent have options. If they don't see a potential for growth or future opportunities, they learn what they can and move on to another organization. Some of your highest performers will leave if you don't help them grow and recognize them for their contribution and innovation.

Fast-Track Your High-Potential Leaders

A few of your high performers also possess a capacity for leadership. These high potentials or "HIPOs" can perform successfully in leadership roles if given the opportunity. Some managers are afraid that if they invest their efforts in growing a high potential, the person will outgrow the team.

Not only is it *possible* to lose the HIPOs you develop, it is *probable* they will be promoted. Your goal is to leverage your high potentials' leadership performance while you have them.

A strong leader knows that developing and influencing a potential leader is good for the organization and part of a manager's job. It is better to contribute to the growth and success of an organization's future leaders than to ignore and lose those talents altogether. Having a friendly leader you helped advance is preferable to competing against one who leaves to work for a rival.

Turbo-Charge High Potentials

To retain HIPOs and maximize their contributions to your team, they must be challenged. Encourage your high potentials to take advantage of:

- On-the-job tasks that expand functions.

- Stretch projects to reach higher outcomes.

- Job transfers, rotations or loans to develop competencies.

- Feedback and coaching.

- Opportunities to "showcase" their talents.

- Mentoring and sponsoring.

- Professional or executive coaching.

- Training programs, including instructor-led, e-learning and self-study.

Observe reactions when you offer additional training and development opportunities. Those who show interest often possess the potential to lead. Those who don't respond may need encouragement or perhaps to be left alone. Some of your high performers may be happy in their current role and/or as an independent contributor without additional leadership commitments.

■   ■   ■   ■   ■

High-Performance Dashboard:
Collaborate & Innovate

The secret to winning results is to have everyone on your team understand, align with and commit to a common purpose and operating practices.

 Gauge how well your team collaborates and innovates by answering below on a scale of 1-5 (5 being highest).

To help drive my team's collaboration and innovation efforts, I

_____ Ensure all members have clear instructions, understand our team's roles and rely on each other.

_____ Encourage team members to reach out to collaborate, to seek knowledge, and to ask for help from others.

_____ Champion my people's ideas and encourage their innovation.

_____ Give members permission to take risks and/or to make mistakes.

_____ Acknowledge and give my people credit for their contributions.

Total **"Collaborate & Innovate" Score (Insert this score on your High-Performance Dashboard on page 57.)**

Your High-Performance Action Plan

To improve my performance score, I need to:

_____

_____

_____

_____

We never stop searching for what we've got to do to turn it back around. Sometimes, you've got to take big steps to turn it around and, sometimes, it's just right there and you're just missing one little ingredient.

– Jeff Gordon,
NASCAR's four-time Sprint Cup
Series champion

Focus On & Produce Winning Results

If you want to motivate team members and increase their focus to produce even better results, create a winning environment. As a leader, you may have the power to address roadblocks and provide assistance in finding resources and freeing your people's availability to work. Performance improves when obstacles are removed, and the right support is provided.

Clear the Path and Provide Assistance

Team members have difficulties focusing on results if their paths aren't clear of complications, delays and interruptions. When possible, limit distractions that slow down work. To keep your people engaged, determine where your assistance is needed. Survey respondents identified changes that would help them focus and produce better results. These are:

- Less red tape and/or bureaucracy.

- Administrative help or additional support staff.

- More flexible hours.

- Additional training and support.

- Reduction of meetings and conference calls.

- Fewer emails, IMs and texts.

More than 80% of people surveyed reported they would be at least 25% more productive if these issues were resolved.

Negotiating Red Tape and/or Bureaucracy

A leader's job is to give the proper tools and instructions and to remove unnecessary roadblocks that hinder getting the job done.

To assist your people in negotiating through organizational curves:

- Help them realistically identify what can and cannot be changed.

- Consider identifying others who are experiencing or have overcome the same types of red tape or organizational roadblocks.

- Determine all the stakeholders and their interests, especially the ones most likely to champion a change, and seek their support.

- Define a benefit for each stakeholder for the change you're proposing.

- Understand what outcomes and goals are being sought.

Provide Assistance With Resources

When people have too much to do and not enough time to do it, they can shut down and accomplish nothing. Many people simply need help with prioritization and deciding what tasks can wait, be delegated or be removed.

Most high performers already know how to prioritize and are accomplishing much more than the average employee. They usually attempt to complete tasks without asking for much help. However, when they do ask for assistance, be open to the request. To find additional support:

- See if all your administrative help is working on priority work.

- Look at team members who may not be fully utilized.

- Check with other teams. If work slows down in one area, someone who already has relevant expertise and knowledge may be available.

- Use temporary help when possible.

This is a good time to negotiate with your team on goals they will commit to meet if given extra help. If you can promise additional results or an improved time frame, you are better prepared to receive a positive response when approaching upper management to seek additional help.

Help Your High Performers Pace Themselves
One obstacle high performers face is self-imposed. Because they accomplish more than others, they have a tendency to take on too much and push themselves too hard. Help them pace themselves and find the help they need before they burn out. Watch for signs of stress or being overwhelmed, such as missed deadlines, reduced communication, increased sick leave or withdrawal.

Provide Additional Training and Development
Return on investment (ROI) is the deciding factor when

organizations prioritize the budget for employee training and development. In our survey, these skills were identified as the most critical to attaining high performance.

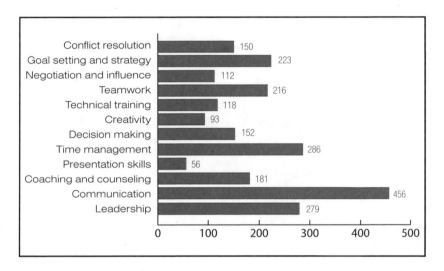

More than half of respondents (456 of 810) identified *communication skills* as the most needed area for training and development. Therefore, when providing any training for high performance, include a focus on communication skills.

Assist With Schedules/Flexible Hours

Flexible work hours are now common practice. Flexibility creates an attachment or loyalty to an organization. If people meet deadlines and are present when duties require them to be, flexibility is reasonable. Ideas for enabling flexibility include:

■ Earlier or later arrival or departure times.

■ Working more hours on certain days.

■ Partial days.

■ Telecommuting from home.

Maximize Performance

Work environments often do not motivate everyone to focus on and produce superior results. One of the biggest obstacles to higher performance is finding available time to work. Instead of working, people keep busy negotiating time wasters, such as meetings, email, voice mail and instant messaging.

Take Action

High performers crave action and completion. One of the worst time wasters is sitting in meetings. Not deciding next steps leads to rehashing issues, creates confusion about actions to be taken and leaves important matters undone. Before ending any meeting, have the group decide open items, assign responsibilities and commit to deadlines.

Stop the Meeting Madness

Mandatory attendance at multiple, time-consuming meetings detours performance. Many organizations have entered into a culture of excessive meetings and conference calls. Indicators of this problem include:

- Holding several pre-meetings to prepare for meetings.

- Meetings with no agendas.

- Participants being forced to attend an entire meeting when only a portion of it is relevant to them.

- Events placed on calendars without approval.

- Abrupt schedule changes.

- Convening big groups when just a few people need to be involved.

Handle Open Items

P   **Park** – Good idea/not good timing.

R   **Reverse** – Something isn't working/more info needed/revisit.

N   **Neutral** – Need to wait to see if a result or action is taken before knowing which way to head.

D   **Drive** – You're ready to go at full speed ahead.

L   **Low gear** – Proceed slowly and observe in case a change is required.

At times, you may have to:

S   **Shift** – Change gears to head in a different direction.

Maximize Your Meetings

Leaders maximize their meetings to drive the best outcomes. To make every minute count:

- Follow rules of engagement for all meetings. (For example, stay on time, restrict use of electronics and limit side discussions.)

- Craft and distribute an agenda ahead of the meeting or as part of the invitation.

- Invite only people who need to be there.

- Decide if anything should be done beforehand.

- Send others with knowledge or delegate attendance, if possible.

- Shorten the meeting time.

- Meet while standing or walking to another event.

- Inquire if you can only attend the portion you are needed.

- Decline a meeting request if possible.

- Meet by phone or virtually instead of face-to-face.

- Prioritize and be realistic about items to be covered.

- Make sure everyone understands all post-meeting "next steps."

Create a Communication Plan

Create a communication plan for your team and yourself. In the plan, let others know your team's guidelines and your preferences for connecting. Establish a conference call, email and IM policy:

- On emails, copy only those affected by the subject.

- Put your desired actions in email subject lines or meeting requests: Review, Respond, Decide and Request.

- Prioritize emails according to importance: High, Regular and Low.

- Notify others the way you wish to correspond internally and externally. Leave a voice message letting people know your schedule or when you will respond to emails that day.

- Inform others of your preferred communication mode. If a matter is an emergency, ask them to text or call your cell. If a matter can wait, request that they email.

- Tell people when you'll be out of the office or the frequency you check voice mails on your business line.

- Replace lengthy email dialogues by instructing team members to call instead. Encourage them to walk down the hall for a face-to-face discussion when possible.

Plan to Perform

Instead of wondering what challenges the day holds, create a plan that motivates people. Concentrate on the areas you can affect to impact results.

To focus your leadership efforts and drive winning results, ask your team about your performance. What answers would you receive if you asked the key members of your team the following:

> *As your leader, what actions could I take to help you focus and produce even better results?*

Your team members' answers may surprise you. The answers can help you focus on areas or behaviors to start, stop, continue and improve.

When asked, "What actions could your leader take to help you focus and produce even better results?" the top responses in our survey were:

- Provide regular and candid feedback.

- Hold others accountable to their commitments.

- Acknowledge and give credit for accomplishments.

Money Not the Main Motivator

High performers are not as driven by money as you might think. Leaders often mistakenly assume that paying more money will result in higher performance. As long as basic needs are met and the organization is paying a competitive wage, money may not be a primary motivator.

In our survey, most people say they won't work a significant additional amount of time, even though they would be paid double their current wage. In fact, 79% of people are not willing to work more than one extra hour per day, including 39% who are not willing or able to work ANY extra hours per day.

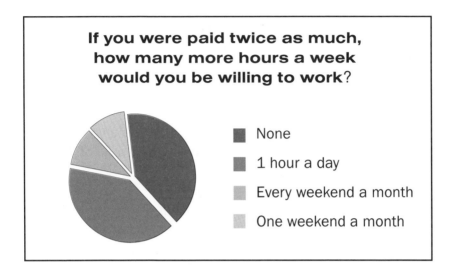

If you were paid twice as much, how many more hours a week would you be willing to work?

- None
- 1 hour a day
- Every weekend a month
- One weekend a month

The hours worked aren't the measure of a team's accomplishment. The true measure of success lies in the results and performance created during those hours. Instead of driving people to work *longer*, help them to work *smarter*.

■ ■ ■ ■ ■

High-Performance Dashboard:
Focus On & Produce Winning Results

The secret to superior results is to listen and offer support. Great leaders help their members focus, work smarter and maximize performance.

 Gauge how well your team focuses on and produces winning results by answering below on a scale of 1-5 (5 being highest).

To help drive focus and produce winning results, I

_____ Help my members negotiate roadblocks and reduce obstacles (such as office politics), bureaucracy/red tape and time wasters.

_____ Gain administrative help or additional support when needed.

_____ Offer additional training and development.

_____ Provide flexible hours or working arrangements when appropriate.

_____ Pace myself and concentrate on my own development and growth.

Total **"Focus On & Produce Winning Results" Score (Insert this score on your High-Performance Dashboard on page 57.)**

Your High-Performance Action Plan

To improve my performance score, I need to:

_____

_____

_____

_____

If you wake up every morning
not wanting to learn something,
you might as well quit this business.

— **Tommy Baldwin, Jr.,**
former crew chief, current owner
of Tommy Baldwin Racing,
a NASCAR team

SUMMARY:

Lead Like a Champion

Race-team leaders know they can't drive a race car consistently at a speed of 200 miles per hour. Your engine burns up, parts stop working correctly and the car and its driver will malfunction. Most leaders know they can't drive their team too hard before problems occur.

You considered your team and how your leadership can improve performance. Now, how are you maintaining your most valuable resource – *you*?

Pace Yourself

Like the race car and like your team members, *you* can't operate at the highest level all of the time. Working at high speed for extended periods of time creates burnout. You may need to slow down to take care of your physical and mental health, to address issues or simply to allow others to catch up.

Pace yourself. Take care of your health and well being. Consider ways to exercise, get enough sleep and eat responsibly to help you operate at your peak performance level. Next, look for ways to gain better control of time wasters and aggravation like unnecessary red tape, an unmanageable meeting schedule or responding to emails, voicemail and IMs.

Perform a Self-Diagnostic
Identify where you drive influence and efficiency best. Spend time strengthening these areas. Then, pinpoint where you experience drag or lower performance than desired and where your skills need a tune-up.

One of the common traps of driven leaders is performing your subordinates' work because you don't want them to leave or burn out. "Protecting" your people by taking on their work or making decisions that should be delegated creates a bottleneck in decision making, which prevents people from growing in experience. Delegate the tasks you should and leave them delegated.

Keep Your Tank Full
As you rise in leadership, you may not receive as many opportunities for your development. To prevent burnout, remember that your personal and professional growth are important. Refuel by attending a workshop, a conference or an association meeting in your field. One leadership development area identified in our survey is communication skills. Consider additional training and development in communicating more effectively.

Beyond family, you should have at least one or two professional support groups. These professional associations or groups can help you network with people in your industry. Some leaders tap into a coach or accountability partner. Others join or create a group of peers to mentor and provide a safe forum to share ideas and challenges.

Final Thoughts

Your success lies in your ability to find and promote people with the right talents and skills. Your team needs understanding, alignment and commitment to a common purpose. Your job is to inspire your people to focus on improvement, negotiate organizational curves, and drive results when possible. Your team members need the ability to trust, collaborate and innovate at a high level. To win this high-performance race, you need the ability to produce and sustain superior results. Most importantly, as a leader, you need to pace yourself and keep your tank full.

■　■　■　■　■

High-Performance Dashboard:
Lead Like a Champion

As a leader, remember that your well-being and maintaining balance are as important as any leadership or team strategy.

 Gauge how well you lead, pace yourself and keep your tank full by answering below on a scale of 1-5 (5 being highest).

To lead like a champion, I

_____ Keep myself in the best physical and mental condition through exercise, eating well and getting enough sleep.

_____ Have addressed or eliminated unnecessary red tape and aggravations to gain more control of my work environment.

_____ Am appropriately delegating work and not taking on my subordinates' work or responsibilities.

_____ Am involved with professional groups that share best practices, provide current information and allow me to network with other professionals.

_____ Select and participate fully in training and professional development programs to grow my skills and strengths.

[ ] **Total "Lead Like a Champion" Score (Insert this score on your High-Performance Dashboard on page 57.)**

Your High-Performance Action Plan

To improve my performance score, I need to:

_____

_____

_____

_____

Your High-Performance Dashboard

Gauge your leadership performance by inserting your five scores below.

Locate High Performers   **Common Purpose & Operating Practices**   **Collaborate & Innovate**

Focus On & Produce Winning Results   **Lead Like a Champion**

Your High-Performance Total Score

Your Driver's Rating

Based on your total score, determine your performance rating:

90-100 = Champion leader. You and your people are turbo charged!

80-89 = You usually obtain results and know the areas that need optimizing.

65-79 = You're passing but other leaders are passing you by.

50-64 = Your people deserve better, and you deserve better from them.

25-49 = You may be too critical, new to leadership or in a difficult position.

To accelerate your efforts and drive an increase in performance, concentrate on your lowest-scoring areas first. To gauge your progress with your team and your leadership, continue monitoring all of these performance areas.

A copy of this dashboard, other performance tools and the high-performance survey noted in this book are found at **DriveHighPerformance.com.**

Your Personal Action Plan

It's time for your leadership tune-up. Based on your reading, reflection and performance rating:

What will you do more of?

_____

_____

_____

What will you do less of?

_____

_____

_____

What will you do more effectively?

_____

_____

_____

■   ■   ■   ■   ■

How to Order This Book

The Manager's
High-Performance
Handbook

To order additional copies of this powerful handbook,
visit **www.walkthetalk.com** or call us at 888.822.9255.
It would be our pleasure to help you with your ordering needs.

For quantity discounts, please email us at
info@walkthetalk.com or call **888.822.9255**.

Other Recommended Management Development Resources

The Manager's Communication Handbook –
This powerful handbook will allow you to connect
with employees and create the understanding,
support and acceptance critical to your success.
It will introduce you to the four key dimensions
of communication and teach you how to eliminate
communication barriers.

The Manager's Coaching Handbook – A must-have
handbook for leaders at all levels. This cut-to-the-
chase resource provides managers, supervisors, and
team leaders with simple, easy-to-follow guidelines for
positively affecting employee performance. Within the
pages, you'll find practical strategies for dealing with
superior performers, those with performance
problems, and everyone in between.

Listen Up, Leader! – Be the type of leader everyone
will follow! This best-selling leadership book
provides powerful insight into what employees want
and need from their managers, supervisors, and team
leaders. It pinpoints the behaviors and attributes
necessary to be the kind of leader that employees
will follow ... to higher levels of success.

To learn more about our hundreds of resources designed to help
managers become more effective and respected leaders,
visit **walkthetalk.com**

About the Author

Linda Byars Swindling is a workplace communication expert. She developed negotiating strategies to drive high performance first as a successful attorney and mediator and later as a keynote speaker, executive coach and strategic consultant. A Certified Speaking Professional (CSP) and president of Journey On, she is the author of *Stop Complainers and Energy Drainers: How to Negotiate Work Drama to Get More Done.* Learn more about Linda Swindling's professional services and resources by visiting her website at **LindaSwindling.com**

Acknowledgements

To my clients, thank you for your help in this project and for allowing me to work with your incredible people. To our survey respondents, thank you for sharing your wisdom so that others may succeed. Thank you to my editing team of Zan Jones, Ginger Shelhimer, Pat and Byron Byars, Jimi Willis, Cathy Rogers and to graphic genius Tim Cocklin. Thanks, Walk the Talk, for the opportunity. Also, a big thanks to my personal pit crew, Gregg, Parker and Taylor, for your unwavering support and routine refueling of food and family fun.

About the Publisher

The Walk the Talk Company

Since 1977, our goal at Walk the Talk has been both simple and straightforward: to provide you and your organization with high-impact resources for your personal and professional success.

We believe in developing capable leaders, building strong communities, and helping people stay inspired and motivated to reach new levels of skills and confidence. When you purchase from us and share our resources, you not only support small business, you help us on our mission to make the world a more positive place.

Each member of the walkthetalk.com team appreciates the confidence you have placed in us, and we look forward to serving you and your organization in the future.

To learn more about us, visit **walkthetalk.com**.

You can drive high performance. Great leaders surround themselves with great people. They have team members who support a common purpose and team-operating practices. High-performing leaders inspire collaboration and innovation. They keep their teams focused and producing superior results. Like you, they invest their time identifying obstacles and developing their strengths.

Congrats and Welcome to the Winner's Circle!

WALKTHETALK.COM

Resources for Personal and Professional Success